FORM & SPACE
IN JAPANESE
ARCHITECTURE

NORMAN F CARVER JR

Books by Norman F. Carver, Jr.
ITALIAN HILLTOWNS
IBERIAN VILLAGES
JAPANESE FOLKHOUSES
SILENT CITIES
NORTH AFRICAN VILLAGES

NORMAN F CARVER JR

FORM & SPACE
IN JAPANESE
ARCHITECTURE

DOCUMAN PRESS LTD

ACKNOWLEDGMENTS

I owe a great deal to all the many persons and institutions that gave me assistance during my stays in Japan: first, the Fulbright Commission for awarding me the study grants and the Fulbright staff in Tokyo and Kyoto; the students and teachers of Kyoto University, particularly Professor Jiro Murata, for their guidance; the Imperial Household Office in Kyoto for granting permission to photograph the great buildings in their charge; the many anonymous and friendly farm families, priests of innumerable temples and shrines with whom we shared a cup of tea; Priest Hagiwara of the Ise Grand Shrine; my good friend Yojiro Yoshimura of Osaka who was so generous in showing his beautiful house; Miss Chieko Kuno for really starting the whole project on its way and to the whole Kuno family for their friendship and their inestimable help; Ryuichi Hamaguchi for his initial interest and encouragement; my wife and children for their help and companionship on travels in Japan; and more recently those who helped pilot this new edition through many editorial and technical problems. To all of them, my deepest gratitude.

Documan Press, Ltd.
Post Office Box 387
Kalamazoo, Michigan 49005
USA

ISBN: 0-932076-10-6 Cloth
ISBN: 0-932076-11-4 Paper

Designed by Norman F. Carver, Jr.
Printed by Dai Nippon
Printed in Japan

CONTENTS

PREFACE

From the several thousand photographs made during nearly three years' study in Japan (1953-55, & 1964) the 214 included in this book have been carefully chosen. In the selection of the photographs and in the accompanying commentary no attempt has been made to cover the whole sweep of Japanese architectural history or to present an exhaustive description of materials and techniques. Meticulous cataloguing of influence and counter-influence, careful tabulation of plan and measured facade, as useful as they are, too often fail to convey the true nature of any architecture. Therefore, I have assumed a basic acquaintance on the part of the reader and gone beyond such particulars to present, instead, insight into the abstract ideas which impelled traditional Japanese architecture and their implications for modern architecture.

Such an approach, of course, is concerned not with fact alone but with interpretation of fact. And it creates the difficult problem of communicating the subtle essences of three dimensional form and space through the two dimensional medium of the printed page. In an attempt to minimize this barrier to understanding I have restricted my written commentary and relied primarily on the uninterrupted flow of visual images, interpretive in their own right.

NFC, Kyoto, 1955 & Kalamazoo 1992

JAPANESE ARCHITECTURE

Almost entirely unknown to the outside world, a brilliant architectural tradition flourished in Japan for more than a thousand years.

Even though its archetypes date from well back into prehistory, we can probably mark the beginnings of this tradition from the founding of Ise Shrine (70) in the 7th century, with its heroically elemental buildings replicating ancient palaces. Reaching a creative zenith in the 17th and 18th centuries it was effectively abandoned in the late 19th, overwhelmed by Japan's sudden contact with the outside world in the 1860's.

Today, all that remains is a legacy of magnificent, aging buildings which, however, continue to exert a powerful influence far beyond their time. This book is an homage to that legacy and to those extraordinarily lucid examples of what I call authentic architecture — architecture which both genuinely reflects and shapes its time and culture.

My book is not a plea for a revival of this great tradition. Rather, amidst the current confusion in contemporary architecture, it is a plea to heed its lessons.

Meaning for Modern Architecture

What we now call Modern Architecture was, originally, an attempt to create a radically new 'style' — to make buildings in the nature of modern man. In the process we architects hoped to discover certain broad principles — those abstractions that approach the essence, "the felt structure of reality" — ideas which could sustain and revitalize indefinitely. Unfortunately, these aims were never realized because, quite simply, Modern Architecture never became truly "modern". Its practitioners and critics too quickly degenerated into the same stylistic dogma and clichés that earlier they so vehemently disparaged.

The first publication of this book in 1955 was, in part, my response to that perceived lapse. This new edition is a modest antidote for the even greater malevolence of the intervening decades. Meanwhile, Modern Architecture's noble aims remain unfulfilled and the many problems go largely unsolved.

Normally, new and perplexing problems cause us to search for some guide to action, first in our own experience and then in the experience of others. The search may even extend across the boundaries of space and time to other cultures, drawing on the collective wisdom of mankind.

Japanese architecture, as one of history's most sophisticated and thoroughly integrated traditions, is such a treasury of architectural wisdom. Moreover, it periodically absorbed vital changes in form, materials, and philosophy from outside, yet maintained its own unique character — a character so ingrained that it shaped everything from simple folk houses to grand temples and aristocratic palaces.

The particular forms and spaces were selected for the book not only because they are visually striking, but also because they illuminate the guiding principles behind this architecture. To me, they seem especially eloquent in awakening the imagination, perhaps for the first time, to a full spectrum of architectural possibilities and principles.

(continued on page 25)

PROLOGUE

Studied compositions of natural elements emphasized intrinsic shapes, patterns, and textures. These were often contrasted with man-made forms to underscore the innate characteristics of each . . .

Daisen-in garden, a detail of the early 1950's restoration, Daitoku-ji, Kyoto (10).

11

*Daisen-in garden detail, plan view of rocks
and white gravel (12). Shinmei-gu, Shinto shrine
in the ancient Ise style (13).*

An appreciation for the expressive power of unadorned form . . .

Water basin and dipper, Yasukuni Shrine, Tokyo (14). Small building at Muro-ji Temple near Nara (15).

Throughout the thousand, often turbulent, years of its development, Japanese architecture maintained an extraordinary continuity, even consistency, in form, materials, technique, and detail. Such consistency extended not only over a·vast time, but also over a wide range of building types — from great shrines and temples to simple farm houses, from elegant palaces and villas to rustic tea pavilions . . .

The Shinmei style Atsuta Shrine, Nagoya, clean and bright after a major restoration typical at Shinto shrines every few decades (16, 17).

The Shoin, main building of the great Katsura Palace, Kyoto (18, 179-194).

Miyajima Shrine near Hiroshima, the entrance corridor (20, 31, 75, 82-94). Tea pavilion at Shugakuin Palace, Kyoto (21, 141, 166-167).

Pavilion and garden, Manshu-in Temple, Kyoto (22, 134-137). Thatch-roofed farmhouse in northern Japan, near Tono (23).

Though only a few castles remain, they were the largest and most spectacular architectural forms in Japan — the one building type which, because of its need to symbolize power and resist assault or fire, bears little resemblance to main stream architecture.

Walls and central towers, Himeji castle, west of Osaka (24).

INTRODUCTION (continued from page 7)

Presenting this ancient tradition from the two primary aspects of space and form helps to clarify the essential organization of each. However, as forms exist only in space and space is always defined and directed by form, in the concept of one the other is always implied.

Form, Space and Image

Abstract concepts such as form, space, pattern, harmony and order, allow us to move beyond particular shapes with their inseparable cultural and emotional associations, and deal instead with relationships and principles. In this way, I feel Japanese architecture becomes intelligible and relevant across the often impenetrable boundaries of time and culture.

My photographs portray a wide variety of building types from the aristocratic tradition — palaces, tea houses, temples, and shrines — and cover a broad scope in time, place, and scale. One essential type not covered here was the subject of a previous book of mine, *Japanese Folkhouses*, which documented the remarkably potent and handsome folk tradition.

Even though photographs cannot completely substitute for the actual encounter with architecture, certain advantages lie within photography's limitations. In the ability to record only a small segment of the total impression lies the advantage of abbreviating to the point of clarity — of pointing out and intensifying the essentials.

In addition, today few buildings or building complexes exist in unspoiled purity, so fragments from many must contribute to establishing a sense of the whole. Though concentrating upon detail, the book's organization makes evident the interrelationships of these details. This attention emphasizes how the ordering of parts contributes to the whole — something that contemporary architects, in haste to evolve their own "significant forms", often overlook.

Appreciation of Japanese architecture in the abstract — in photographs devoid of a sense of function and cultural connections — is possible because its patterns and rhythms project their own articulation on the observer, generating an energy and tension to which the mind reacts directly.

Appreciation is heightened with the realization that this architecture has an intrinsic functional, cultural basis — that individual buildings were part of a wider framework, a framework shaped by a way of life which it both contained and implemented.

The drawings at the right show a few of the basic house types from prehistoric times until the present. Remains of such pit houses have been excavated in several locations, and similar shelters still exist on the grounds of Ise Shrine. The elevated structures apparently were used as granaries, houses and eventually as palaces. Its use for the very sacred Ise Shrine seems to confirm this form was reserved for special purposes. For both traditional and practical purposes later house types continued the practice of raised floors.

PREHISTORIC PIT HOUSE

PREHISTORIC RAISED GRANARY/HOUSE

PALACE/SHRINE, ISE STYLE 8TH CENT

RESIDENCE, 19TH CENTURY

EVOLUTION OF THE JAPANESE HOUSE

FORM IN JAPANESE ARCHITECTURE

The idea of form in architecture embraces more than simply exterior shape or configuration. Architectural form includes all aspects of spatial form, from visible shape, color, and texture to internal structure. Moreover, the word "form" when applied to architecture implies an organic unity and intrinsic harmony of all its elements — the implication that in form we perceive an ordered, coherent whole.

Japanese Architecture and Order

Of all the principles discernible in Japanese architecture, the most visible is a pervasive sense of order. It is an order so thorough and yet so innately flexible and energizing that its integration of the inherent complexities of form and space appears almost effortless. It is this revelation of an all-embracing order that may be the most important lesson of Japanese architecture.

Order, of course, indicates a unifying idea which relates complex elements either visually or conceptually. Rigid axial symmetry is a common ordering technique often found in religious and official structures both in Japan and the West. Such symmetry is visually obvious, readily applied, easily comprehended, and conveys a sense of monumentality and power.

Despite its effectiveness, however, symmetry imposes severe restraints on form. A building's functions seldom arrange easily in a neat symmetry — especially when the building houses diverse uses or evolves over several generations.

In contrast, Japanese folk houses, for example, free of aesthetic pretense and often impelled by dire necessity, exhibited a natural irregularity of form. To accommodate varied functions farmers added or extended rooms, shifted beams and columns, or freely inserted windows and doors. In fact, it was this peasant tradition of informality and asymmetry, idealized by influential tea masters and appropriated for everything from tea houses to princely villas, that inspired the dominant aesthetic of Japan's architectural golden age.

Order and Asymmetry

Perfection of a system of asymmetrical order may be Japan's most significant contribution to architecture. For, in contrast with symmetry, the inherent vitality of asymmetry requires participation in the experience of form — by suggesting, by directing the mind to complete the incomplete, and by providing a constant source of ever-changing relationships in space. Asymmetrical order is not an externally imposed finality, but an extension of the process of life. Asymmetry recognizes that life is not static or perfectible, but that its essence is growth, change, relatedness.

Structure and Form

Rampant informality, however, was restrained by the structural network, inherently rational and regular. The visual expression of structure's integral geometry and rhythms not only helped organize and restrain overall form, but also permeated the architecture to create a rigorous unity even to the smallest detail. The harmony of colors and textures of natural materials further enhanced this sense of unity.

The consequence was an architecture indivisible from Japanese life — a genuine expression of a civilization's impulse to form.

From ancient times an elemental, direct structure, boldly expressed, has been the fundamental basis of form . . .

FORM

Shinmei-gu Shrine near Matsumoto is similar
to the ancient Ise forms, where prominent
structural elements became distinctive symbols of
the style (30). Great tree-trunk shafts rise from
the floor of the bay to form the torii arch of
Miyajima (31, 82).

From ancient times the pillar has had special significance in Japanese architecture. It was, after all, a powerful symbol — the very act of raising a pillar symbolized the will to build, affirmed one's existence, and marked a place where man, not nature, was in control.

Early religious forms incorporated this symbolism directly by the use of huge columns — some standing free of the walls and rising out of the ground to the very peak of the roof. Such forms continue today in shrine buildings of the Ise style.

This veneration of the elemental pillar meant that structure — especially the forthright expression of structural forces and patterns — became a prime determinant of Japanese architectural form.

Archaic buildings tended to be dense and interior spaces small and utilitarian. As building skills developed, however, and functional needs grew, the structure thinned and expanded into a loose cage-like system. This flexible post and beam system, inspired increasingly larger interior spaces linked to each other and to the exterior.

The reliance on wood structural members — straight timbers for posts and beams — meant that, except for the most primitive buildings, complex forces logically resolved into their vertical and horizontal components. Thus, the rectangular geometrical order of the post and beam system underlying Japanese architecture was not an arbitrarily imposed geometry, but structurally and rationally derived.

Mountainside temple building at Muro-ji, south of Nara. The splendidly rhythmic supports for a temple platform (32-33).

Temple structures built on the mountainside at Sanbutsu-ji, at Misasa near Tottori (34-35).

The sub-structure beneath the huge sloping roofs of farm houses or temples followed the same rectilinear system. A few large timbers supported a web of smaller members, often resulting in impressive, cathedral-like spaces.

Myoho-in, detail of roof structure, Kyoto (36). Sunlight streaming through openings high above the entrance at Nanzen-ji, Kyoto (37).

The structural system served not only the practical requirements of overall form, it was also the source of the form's modular order, its rhythmic complexities, and ultimately, its unique beauty.

In other words, the mere statement of structural fact was not the final intent — structure was not always straight-forward, exposed and logical. Apparent structural elements were freely added or manipulated for their rhythmic decorative effects and others, such as diagonal bracing, deliberately hidden.

Main hall of the Sasagawa house, a large farm house at Mikata in northern Japan (38).

Store houses at Kamigamo Shrine, Kyoto (39t) and Toshodai-ji, Nara (39m) use an interesting wall-bearing technique with similar structural expressiveness. In this abandoned farm building (39b), the basic construction system is clearly shown — posts directly supporting the major horizontal beams, infill walls of mud plaster over bamboo lath, and horizontal or diagonal bracing buried in the plaster walls.

The Japanese intuitively recognized that the perception of form is essentially a pattern making function. The structural necessities of spatial form, therefore, were gradually transformed into dynamic patterns and radiating rhythms that helped unify and order the total form.

As a result the conjunction of contrasting materials, elements, or forces was a vital means of expression. Here, in these seemingly mundane events of architecture, the overall order was given the added depth of eloquent and meaningful relationships — the strong dark column and the thin white wall, for example, convey their true meanings of support and non-support. Each element has its own existence stated clearly, yet always with a sense of value beyond itself — a sense of the spiritual emanating from the material and the universal reflected in the particular. . .

Mondrian-esque facade of Myoshin-ji Temple, Kyoto (40-41).

*Beautifully proportioned structural patterns —
a temple at Takao, Kyoto (42), Horyu-ji near
Nara (43t), Tofuku-ji, Kyoto (43b).*

44

More structural patterns at Tofuku-ji, Kyoto (44t) and Horyu-ji, Nara (44b, 45).

45

Details of outer structures at Kasuga Shrine, Nara (46t), and Hiei-jinja Shrine, Sakamoto (46b). Detail of the base of the Junjokan at Daigo-Samboin (47, 71).

Walls with variations on a similar theme at Nijo Castle, Kyoto (48, 49).

Rows of freestanding columns are among the most visible and dramatic features of these bold structural systems.

The Seiryo-den of the Kyoto Imperial Palace or Kyoto Gosho (50t, 50b). Structural patterns in the gate at Ninna-ji Temple, Kyoto (51).

Sankei-en Villa, a former private estate, Yoko-hama (52). Covered passageway at Miyajima Shrine, near Hiroshima (53, 82-94).

The fine-scale functional elements —
windows, doors, grills, railings, for example
— both reflect the large-scale structural
patterns and are imaginatively integrated into
its rigorous geometry.

*Veranda railing details, Keage-jinja, near the
Nanzen-ji temple, Kyoto (54) and the shrine in
front of Yakushi-ji Temple, near Nara (55).*
*Wedged post and beam connection at Takao,
Kyoto (56). Interlocking stone and wood joint
used to repair a post at Honen-in, Kyoto (57).*

The ever-present wood grills add delicate rhythms to the facades, while giving a measure of privacy to the interiors. Such grills were especially common and useful in old Kyoto's narrow streets.

House in Shimabara, Kyoto (58l). Intersection of veranda post, rails and beams, Kamakura-gu, main shrine, Kamakura (58r).

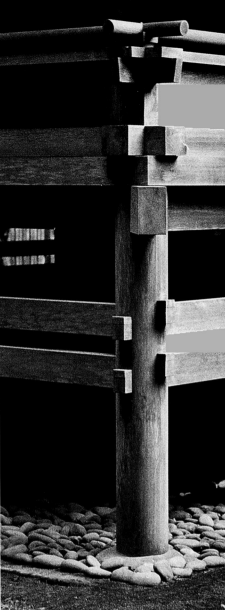

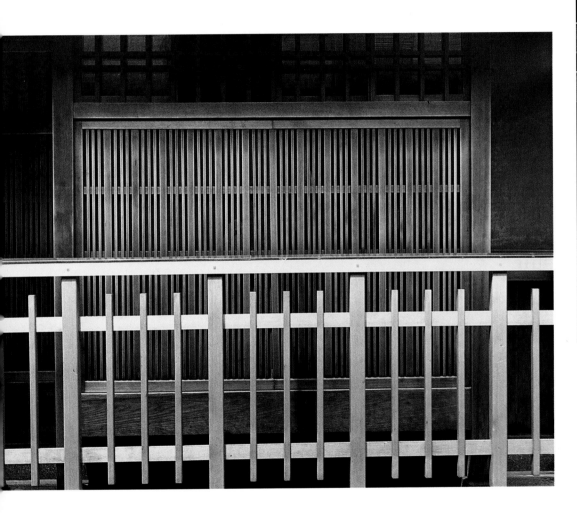

Detail of the front wall of a wealthy farmer's house, Yoshimura-tei, near Osaka (59).

Private house (60t), and tea house of the Nomura Garden (60b), patterns of grills and shoji from the interior.

Detail of a bamboo fence, Katsura Villa, Kyoto (61t). Bamboo-covered wall of a house in Akasaka, Tokyo (61b).

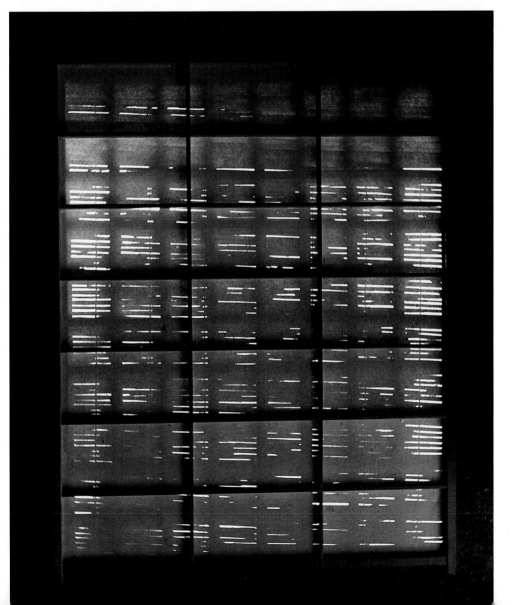

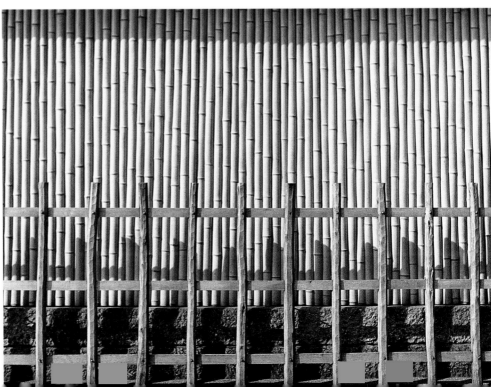

The predominance of natural colors and textures helps establish continuity with nature. Textures, also, give clues to scale and provide tactile and close-range visual interest. Rough, irregular natural elements often are deliberately contrasted with the smooth regularity of the man-made.

Stone and plaster wall at the Tokyo Imperial Palace (62). Raked gravel and paving textures at Ryoan-ji, Kyoto (63t), and at the Nunnery of Hokkei-ji, near Nara (63b).

Entrance to the ceremonial tea house at Manshu-in, Kyoto (64). Typical of tea house doors and windows, a similar exuberant asymmetry occurs at Katsura's Shokin-tei (204).

The intricate, proliferating patterns and planes are contained and unified by the powerful horizontals of the earth and the roof . . .

Country temple, Saitama province (65).

Shoiken tea pavilion in winter (66) and the Shoin (67), Katsura, Kyoto. Examples of how wide overhangs and strong roof lines can visually organize the complex elements below.

Perhaps in no other architectural tradition is the roof as important or produced in such a variety of shapes. Unlike most Western architectural styles, in which the wall dominates and the roof is hardly visible, both wall and roof are important in Japanese architecture. Historically its prominence made the roof a symbol of wealth and position — as much effort and expense could be expended on the roof as on the rest of the building.

However, the roof plays a contradictory role in Japanese architectural composition. Primarily, of course, it visually and psychologically implies the felt limits of shelter. Moreover, its dominant presence helps to unify and order the complex forms it shelters. This very dominance, though, especially when exaggerated by massiveness or vivid decoration, often causes the roof to become a separate and unrelated entity.

The roof's basic shape was determined by established tradition, aesthetics or the desire to impress — as well as more practical considerations. In addition, there were endless options in detail and decoration. For example, the weathering surface might include one or more of the following: the heavy, thick thatch of farm houses, thin wood shingles favored in the palaces, or various styles of clay tile.

Many Japanese roofs have a wonderful hovering quality due to their huge overhangs, sweeping curves, and thin or nearly invisible supports. Practically, the arrangement of columns and wide overhangs permitted great freedom in ordering the space below as forms move in and out effortlessly.

Shokin-tei tea pavilion of Katsura illustrates how the roof can both overpower the composition and order the complex forms which it shelters (68-69).

The main sanctuary of the Naiku complex at Ise, based on ancient house forms (70). Thatched roof of the Junjokan at Daigo-Samboin Temple, near Kyoto (71). The thatch gives these roofs a massiveness which adds to their monumentality.

Ceremonial building (72) and the main shrine of Kashihara-jingu, near Nara (73). Rising and sweeping eaves visually lighten these roofs and expose an underside rich in detail.

Outstanding examples of roof projections handsomely proportioned to the building's height as well as the visual importance of the extended verandas in relation to the overhang. Ninna-ji Temple, Kyoto (74, 129-131). Cere-monial hall of Miyajima Shrine, (75, 82-94).

The conscious use of repetitive roof forms is a favorite design technique . . .

The Kyoto Gosho Palace (76). Myoshin-ji as seen from the Reiun-in (77).

Izumo Shrine near Matsue (78t). Shinmei-gu Shrine near Matsumoto (78b, 13, 30). Tile and thatch roofs of the Hasshokan Inn, Nagoya (79).

Groups of huge thatch roofs, such as these in Tamba near Kyoto, until recently were a common sight in the countryside (80).

This small boathouse at the edge of Shugakuin's pond has a cedar shingle roof held down with tied bamboo poles — elaboration of a technique borrowed from farmers' huts (81).

The great Shinto shrine of Miyajima is built over the waters of a small bay. Appearing to float on the sea at high tide, its many buildings, dance platforms, and connecting galleries, all painted red, are a spectacular sight. Miyajima's large size and complexity make it a superb example of the ordering power of structure.

The great camphor tree torii, symbolic entrance to the shrine, stands far out in the bay (82). Views towards the torii along the central axis from the covered pavilion (83t) and the outdoor platform (83b), used for the dances traditional at Shinto shrines.

A view through the array of supporting columns of the open galleries (84). The Harai-den hall from the central platform (85).

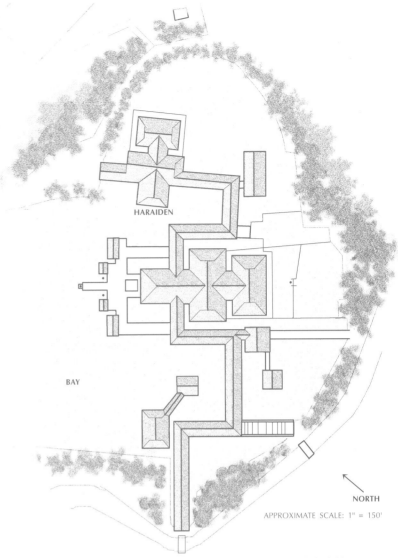

HARAIDEN

BAY

NORTH

APPROXIMATE SCALE: 1" = 150'

M I Y A J I M A   S H R I N E   S I T E   P L A N

More properly known as Itsukushima Shrine, after the name of the small island on which it is located, Miyajima has ancient roots at this site. The present buildings, however, are the result of many rebuildings and the constant renewal required by the ravages of tides, typhoons, and hordes of visitors.

The plan of the Shrine, as might be expected of a religious edifice, is loosely axial, but the multiplicity of buildings and galleries mask this symmetry. It is the vivid and regular structural rhythms which march through these complex forms and spaces, which both unify and give Miyajima its special beauty.

Buildings and galleries at the eastern entrance and the great torii (86-87).

The main Shrine buildings and platforms from
the entrance (88) and a detail of the same area
(89). The roofs play an important part in visually
unifying these complex patterns and forms.

Within the broad structural outlines, additional elements create sub-patterns — the interplay of these small scale rectangular rhythms visually enriches both form and space.

"Floating" pavilions at high tide (90t). At low tide the supports of stone and wood beneath the corridors (90b). Grilled screen walls (91).

The covered galleries are the connecting links at Miyajima (92-93).

A boldly expressed structure establishes the underlying rhythms and proportions which then help integrate and harmonize the myriad details.

The extraordinarily handsome result in the galleries of Miyajima (92-95).

From the standpoint of form and space, Japanese castles are a spectacular accomplishment; however, their construction was a relatively short-lived phenomenon and they had little influence on the main-stream architectural styles.

Castles were erected throughout Japan, largely as a defense against the newly introduced firearms, during the 16th century's endless struggles. Though their primary purpose was defensive, their use as highly visible symbols of power and wealth may have been equally important.

The castles' lower walls and foundations are stone masonry, but the upper portions are mainly constructed of wood covered with thick fire-proofing plaster. This technique enabled the great heights, the exotic silhouettes, and the elaborate details which give castles their unique character.

Matsumoto Castle and moat (97), Tokyo Imperial Palace (98-99). The most spectacular of Japan's remaining castles, Himeiji, southwest of Osaka on the Inland Sea (96, 100-108, 24).

Little remains of the Tokyo Castle, except the extensive outer ramparts and moats in the middle of down-town Tokyo (98-99).

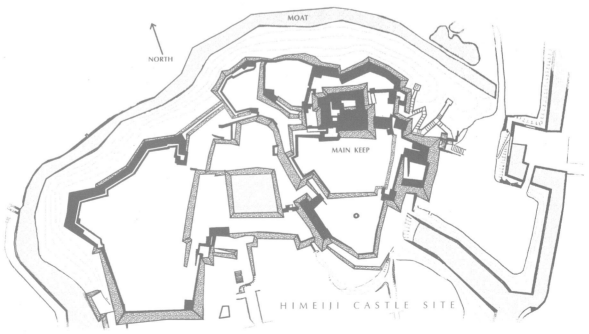

MOAT

NORTH

MAIN KEEP

HIMEIJI CASTLE SITE

Himeiji Castle, overall view of the central keep and subsidiary buildings (100). A model of the fully restored complex reveals the impressive scale of the original fortifications (101t). For defensive purposes the main passage, as might be expected, is full of twists and turns and frequent gates (101b).

The formidable, but strikingly beautiful outer walls of Himeiji (102-103).

104

The many-storied main keep includes a few interior spaces of reasonable size. Detail of the tower (104), the audience chamber (105t), and a fortified door way (105b).

The many roof levels provide ample
opportunity for indulgence in rhythmic arrays of
tiled roofs — handsome from above (106), or
below (107-108). In contrast with the castles'
deadly serious purpose, the result was
picturesque to the extreme.

*This small beautifully proportioned belfry
houses the largest cast bell in Japan -- more than
70 tons. The massive structure resists the bell's
weight and swaying when rung. Enhanced by the
articulation of each member, the belfry is a superb
example of the integration of function, structure
and form. Chion-in Temple, Kyoto.*

SPACE IN JAPANESE ARCHITECTURE

The concept of space in architecture embodies not only the enclosed or interior areas of a building, but also its exterior domains, its site and attendant landscape. The concept also includes the felt qualities of space — for example, its lightness or darkness, oppressiveness or expansiveness, its sense of movement or repose.

Architecture is the art of organizing forms to bring amorphous space to life, making it 'real', perceptible, and useful.

Traditional Japanese architecture, more limited in scale than Western architecture, did not produce the soaring majesty of a Chartre, the remote splendor of a Parthenon, or the overwhelming scale of a Versailles. Japanese spaces, whether civic or private, consistently tended to a more human scale and often made nature an essential part of the composition. Despite such historical disparities, Modern Architecture in the West arrived at spatial concepts concerning the unity and continuity of space remarkably parallel, if not similar, to those of traditional Japanese architecture.

The Development of Space

Sophisticated spaces, however, played little role in the earliest Japanese architecture. Ancient houses, for example, were essentially one-room bulwarks against the elements. Even primitive shrines simply stood in hallowed space, but, as we still can see at Ise, they seldom enclosed significant space. To these early builders, forms tangible, immediate and real were of primary concern. Space, if it existed at all, was merely implied. The idea of space as an indispensable element in the composition developed slowly. It would be many centuries before the Zen masters declared that the essence of a tea cup lay not in the cup itself, but in its emptiness — in its "space".

Over time, Japan's primitive indigenous forms and structural techniques became infused with the radical, liberating ideas, which arrived periodically from the Asian mainland. The expanded vocabulary of forms enabled spaces of increasing virtuosity and complexity.

Motivating Forces

Several critical forces drove this spatial evolution: the practical demands of climate and proliferating functional needs of society, the aesthetic conceits of poetry and painting, and the philosophical insights of changing religious influences.

Of all these forces, undoubtedly the most demanding were climate and the need for ever larger, more varied spaces. Since most architectural innovation took place in the region around the old capitals of Nara and Kyoto — a climate of hot, humid summers and cool, damp winters — buildings developed wide overhanging roofs for protection against typhoon-driven rain and blazing sun. The post and beam structural system supporting these huge roofs allowed great flexibility in space arrangements, as well as movable walls that permitted complete shuttering or maximum openness to cooling breezes.

Sliding partitions between interior supporting posts (*fusuma*) also partially solved the desire for larger rooms otherwise limited by the supporting posts of the ubiquitous wood structural system.

Opening up interiors to the outside was initially a practical solution to problems of comfort and utility, but it also encouraged a fundamental change in direction for Japanese architecture. Space became a major focus and, reinforced by an aboriginal religion of nature-worship, the connection between building space and nature a dominant theme.

As buildings expanded in size, the difficulty of making this connection to the garden and of providing light and air to interior spaces grew geometrically. One handsome and popular solution, clearly illustrated by the Shoin of Katsura (180), joined several smaller structures in a staggered arrangement that permitted maximum exposure of exterior walls. The resulting forms were increasingly complex and, not incidentally, picturesque.

The aesthetics of literature and painting encouraged this picturesqueness. Ink paintings' images and blank expanses also stimulated architecture by creating a very real desire for the empty spaces , lonely hermitages, and misty vistas portrayed in the paintings.

Literature's influences arose from attempts to recreate in concrete form certain common themes in Japanese poetry — themes on nature and the seasonal moods. Rooms were added to take advantage of special views or to enjoy particular seasons. Gardens were even created to match purely fictional descriptions — as apparently occurred at Katsura, where a garden resembles one in the famous 11th century novel, *Tale of Genji*.

Space and Zen

Zen Buddhism, which influenced so many other aspects of culture, provided the philosophical underpinnings for this evolving mix of ideas. Upon Zen's arrival in Japan, it found a similarity between naive beliefs and sophisticated doctrine that resulted in Zen's extensive influence on Japanese art and life. These ideas spread throughout the upper classes influencing their art, poetry, religion and life. At the same time, however, the Zen tea masters began adopting certain aspects of folk culture. As exemplified in the Katsura Villa (178), Japanese architecture flourished during this period by combining aristocratic elegance with the invigorating ancient beliefs preserved in the folk tradition.

Under Zen, space assumed a dominant role in Japanese art. This attitude was strengthened by two important Zen concepts: first, the primacy and reality of immediate experience, and second, the indivisibility of this experience from a present defined as "the moving infinity" — a oneness with life in eternal flux.

This was movement or change that could not be arrested, but only guided —movement through space that could not be confined, but only directed. Space, therefore, became the only true essential, for only in space was movement possible. Space was the universal medium through which life moved in constant transformation, in which place and time were only relative.

Such spatial concepts encouraged concern for the small, human scale events in Japanese architecture and the desire to relate these to a greater whole. Architecture defined the individual's relationships to this spatial-temporal continuity by establishing an ordered progression from the near and precise to the distant and indefinable.

Space is made "real" by its definition: forms, natural and man-made, define spaces that are palpable, singular and yet part of the continuum. A key element in this spatial definition is structure, which by staking out the coordinates, outlines and suggests the essential geometric order of architectural space . . .

S P A C E

Jiko-in, a temple on a low hill in the countryside near Nara. With sliding wall panels removed, the interior space extends not only to the immediate garden, but to the rice fields and hills beyond (113-114).

Architecture developed within and beyond the structural cage as a series of rhythmic patterns and planes of reference, precisely defining portions of continuous space...

Kasuga Shrine outbuildings, Nara (116-118).

117

Ceremonial dance platform and outer walls of Shimo-gamo Shrine, Kyoto (119).

Punctuated by the structural rhythms, wall planes and screens seem to float in space directing movement and views — their asymmetry implying relationships beyond themselves to give space the feeling of infinite extendability . . .

High windows that filter daylight through the dramatic structure make the Kusukabe house interior one of the most impressive in Japan. Takayama. (120, 121).

Shokin-tei tea house, Katsura Palace, Kyoto (122, 200-214). Interior of Shoin, Katsura Palace, Kyoto (123, 180-194).

*Tea house of the Saiho-ji or Moss Garden
Temple, Kyoto (124-125, 168-169).*

Kyoto Gosho Palace, Ko-gosho and adjacent buildings (126-127).

126

Kyoto Gosho Palace, detail of Shishinden complex (128).

Regal in scale and beauty, Ninna-ji Temple, was once known as the Omuro Palace because of historical ties to the Imperial family (129-131).

The outward flow of asymmetrical
rhythms — from architecture's stark geometry
to the free and infinite rhythms of the rocks,
the trees and the mountains . . .

The meeting of architecture and nature is a key to spatial expression. Even though intimately linked to the site by its openness, broad overhangs and extended verandas, the building's precise geometry and slight elevation keep it distinct and separate. Instead of a dramatic interpenetration of interior and exterior, subtle indications of movement between the two express space as one and continuous . . .

Arisawa villa, Matsue (132-133, 158-159).

Wide verandas (roka) extend the interior space, moderate transition to the gardens, as well as relate the building more precisly to the ground. Moving around these pavilions reveals their amazing transparency and the rhythm of repetitive forms (134-135). Manshu-in Temple, Kyoto (134-137).

*Temple garden, near Kyoto (138). Sankei-en,
former private villa, Yokohama (139).*

Gardens, whether large or small, become an integral part of the architectural composition by enhancing form and extending interior space . . .

Daigo-Samboin Temple tea house and garden, Kyoto (140). Shugakuin Palace, upper pavilion with view of mountains in distance. Kyoto (141).

Sites of great natural beauty were highly prized and the more intimate the relationship between a site and the building the better. If interesting natural sites were not available they were created — huge boulders moved, miniature mountains constructed, and distant streams diverted.

Shokin-tei Tea Pavilion of Katsura on its artificially created site beside a pond (145, 200-216). A rest house alongside a stream that tumbles down the eastern slope of Mt. Hiei, near Sakamoto (146). The temple approaches at Takao, outside Kyoto, pass through a grove of majestic trees (147 - 149).

An essential part of any site is a carefully planned entrance. Seldom straight or direct, the routes employ corners, stairways and more often than not a meander, in order to obscure the destination until the very end...

The entrance to Kasuga Shrine, Nara, is lined with stone lanterns, an impressive sight when ablaze on festival evenings (150). The many-angled, multi-level, and variously paved path to Chion-in Temple in Kyoto's eastern hills (151).

The staccato rhythms of steps and columns mark one's progress along the covered passageways at the Nigatsu-do main temple, Nara (152), and the Hasedera near Nara (153).

One does not stride casually along these paths; they are intentionally arranged for deliberate passage, frequent pauses, and with patterns to please the eye.

Garden paths of the Arisawa villa, Matsue (154, 155t), Private garden, Kyoto (155b).

Stepping stones across the ponds of a private garden (156) and of Heian Shrine (157), Kyoto.

Not only the paths themselves, but details along the way, invite a contemplative pause. A constant in many details is the studied contrast of natural and man-made forms.

Stone and bamboo path at the Arisawa villa, Matsue (158, 159). Paths and garden details, Kyoto Gosho (160, 161b), Stone basin in garden of Daitoku-ji Temple, Kyoto (161t).

The garden opposite the Shokin-tei, Katsura.
Unlike gardens composed for viewing from one
or two points, Katsura's landscape invites
wandering with many enchanting vistas (162,
163, 205-216)

Shugakuin Imperial Villa, Kyoto. This large strolling garden combines distant mountain views across a large pond, leafy bowers, and small pavilions half-hidden on the hillsides (166). The path crosses this gently curved bridge, a popular feature in many gardens. Here newly restored, this wooden bridge, surprisingly, supports a gravel walk bordered with moss (164 - 165).

Shugakuin Villa, summer pavilion overlooking the pond of the upper garden (166). Poles support the branches of this picturesque pine overhanging the pond at Heian Shrine (167).

An ancient garden famed for its natural and uncontrived beauty is the Moss Garden or Saiho-ji, outside Kyoto. The handsome wall along the entrance walk (168b), gives no hint of what lies inside. The moss and moss-covered rocks in the upper garden (168t), the grove and pond of the main garden (169, 124-125).

In contrast with strolling gardens, the austere gardens associated with Zen temples were usually composed for viewing from one location — a special room or an adjacent veranda. Simple and restrained, they may consist merely of several carefully selected and meticulously arranged rocks, raked sand, and a few plants. The scale of these gardens, intentionally ambiguous, alternates between the immediate and the infinite.

Garden of Nanzen-ji (170), and Daitoku-ji, Kyoto (171, 10)

The most famous and abstract of these gardens, Ryoan-ji, is approached through a dark temple interior. Suddenly a brilliant white rectangle appears. Stone groupings gradually emerge from the glare — then imperceptibly, the scale shifts as the stones become distant islands on a shimmering sea.

Ryoan-ji Temple garden, Kyoto (172 - 175).

These may be the most carefully studied fifteen stones in the world. Though arranged primarily for viewing from the temple veranda, relationships between groups are intriguing from any angle. In the background, the wall has been long admired for the painterly patina of its weathered surface. Ryoanji details (174, 175).

The desire for an ordered landscape manifests itself in the rice paddies of the countryside.

Flooded rice fields in Tamba, just west of Kyoto (176-177).

Behind this simple fence on the outskirts of Kyoto lies the Katsura Villa, the extraordinary masterpiece of Japanese architecture.

Construction of Katsura began during the early 17th century at a time when Japanese aesthetics, inspired by Zen and the cult of tea, became infused with the energy and ideals of the peasant classes. A sensitive prince, with the help of the most talented builders and tea masters of his time, by sheer audacity and inventiveness broke free of stifling aristocratic traditions. They transformed earlier vague ideas of form and space, achieving a degree of originality and perfection seldom seen before or since.

Katsura consists of a large stroll garden and pond, several small tea pavilions, and the main palace or Shoin. A path linking the buildings, meanders through a garden of intimate alcoves, expansive lawns, rocky inlets, and breathtaking vistas.

The simple, rustic tea pavilions, reminiscent of farm houses, blend quietly with the background. In contrast, the Shoin, elevated, abstract and elegant, seems to float above its site. It was built in three parts — now called the Old Shoin, the Middle Shoin, and the New Palace or New Shoin. Unifying this whole composition is a pervasive sense of balance and repose, enhanced by an all-embracing nature.

In many ways Katsura is the culmination of centuries of evolution in Japanese architecture. Perhaps it is the only place where, because of the exceptional clarity and range of expression, one can discover the essence of form and space in Japanese architecture.

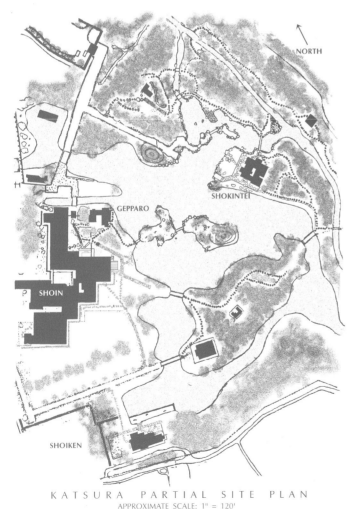

NORTH

SHOKINTEI

GEPPARO

SHOIN

SHOIKEN

KATSURA PARTIAL SITE PLAN
APPROXIMATE SCALE: 1" = 120'

Katsura Villa and gardens (178-216, also 18, 66-68, 122-123, 145, and 162-163).
The bamboo and reed fence surrounding part of the Katsura grounds (178). Pond and rocks of the central garden opposite the Shoin (179).

The unusual height and staggered plan of the Shoin gives each major room access to sunlight and a splendid view of the gardens — and not incidentally, echoes a style much in vogue at the time, the irregular profile likened to wild geese in flight.

From the foreground, the New Shoin, the terrace of the Music Room, the Middle Shoin, and Old Shoin (180). East wall of the New Shoin (181).

*Detail of the Middle Shoin (182) and the
south facade of the New Shoin (183).*

Roof forms and structure echo along the stepped facades of the Shoin (184, 185) — the black and white patterns enhanced by a rare Kyoto snowstorm (184).

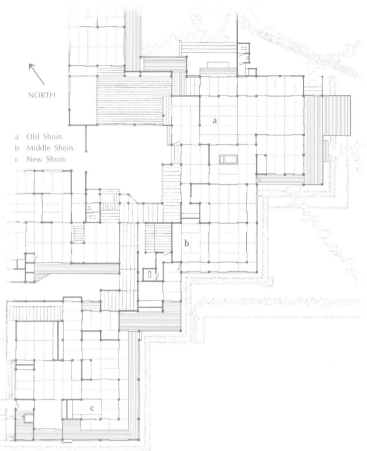

S H O I N ,   P A R T I A L   P L A N
SCALE: 1" = 30'   SEE PAGE 218 FOR COMPLETE PLAN

a Old Shoin
b Middle Shoin
c New Shoin

NORTH

The rectangular asymmetry of the exterior relentlessly orders the interior. There rhythmic planes and bold geometry articulate complex structural and practical needs, resulting in a space that is nearly abstract and seemingly infinite.

Interior of Old Shoin looking south to the corner of the Middle Shoin. To the right of the opening is an alcove or tokonoma *for display of flower arrangements and scroll paintings. The flexibility of interior* fusuma *and exterior* shoji *sliding panels allows an infinite combination of spaces and openings to the garden (186-187).*

187

The Old Shoin, looking to the interior from the corner of the tokonoma (188). New Shoin veranda, with outer shoji closed (189) — the space behind the facade shown on (181). Indicative of changing tastes are the overly elaborate details of this late addition compared with those of the earlier Shoins.

Extensions of architectural elements and patterns into the landscape enhance the link between interior and exterior space...

Open veranda of the Middle Shoin with the moss and stones below echoing the zigs and zags of the plan (190, 191).

Moon-viewing deck of the Old Shoin and the beautifully proportioned three-dimensional facade of which it is a part — from inside (192), from across the Pond (193), and also (67).

The interplay between irregular landscape and precise geometry accentuates the inherent characteristics of each and creates a wonderful contrapuntal harmony throughout Katsura...

Old Shoin, West facade detail (194). Stepping stones penetrate deeply under the eaves of the Shoiken tea pavilion (195, 196).

The tea pavilions of Katsura display an aspect of Japanese architecture quite different from the Shoin. Deriving their aesthetics from the farm houses so much admired by the tea masters, they are much less formal and austere, richer and more natural in textures and colors. Yet these deceptively rustic forms enclose spaces of amazing sophistication . . .

Shoiken, entrance facade and stepping stones (195, 196) and interior (197).

196

The Gepparo tea pavilion includes two raised tatami-floored rooms overlooking the garden, and a large earth-floored space completely open on one side (198, 199).

Despite its modest size and humble materials — meant to evoke the appearance of a lonely hermitage — the Shokin-tei is among the noblest, most sophisticated works in the history of architecture.

Except for the great hovering roof, it seems to exist not so much in space as to be of space — its form so transparent and ephemeral, that the interior and the garden merge imperceptibly to create that ideal sensation of one continuum.

The Shokin-tei tea pavilion and the nearby garden (200-215, 68, 122, 145, 162-163).

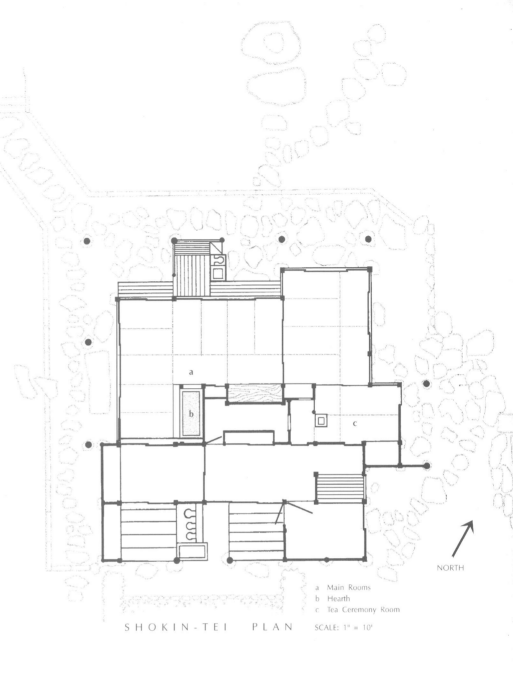

a Main Rooms
b Hearth
c Tea Ceremony Room

SHOKIN-TEI   PLAN   SCALE: 1" = 10'

NORTH

Thin, frail planes, advancing and receding in space, create ever-changing relationships and a sense of impermanency, continuity, and movement — expressing the tea masters' philosophy that life, after all, is fleeting and mere illusion.

Main rooms of the Shokin-tei from the western opening. The blue checked pattern at first seems out of place, but in its intense abstraction of the building's geometry, it almost becomes the secret source from which Katsura's rectilinear rhythms emanate (202-203).

203

The studied asymmetry of the tea ceremony room exterior with its ritual crawl-through entrance (204-206). The garden approach across the stone bridge, (205, 212).

The art of asymmetry and its engaging
energy is nowhere more magical or profound
than in the Shokin-tei.

Movement, actual or implied, is of the essence. These gardens are not static spaces with but a single viewpoint. They are intended to be seen by strolling the paths, pausing occasionally to enjoy a vista, to discover a composition of stones, or to glimpse the half-hidden roof of a tea house. In other words, to constantly experience movement, change, and discovery.

The architecture, open and slight, shelters a mere fragment of continuous space. The implied link of interior and landscape is abbreviated and subtle, encouraging the imagination in grasping the whole. There is less a projection of architectural geometry than a sense of flow beginning in the free asymmetry of the interior planes and ending in the echoing rhythms of great boulders looming in the garden.

Images of the Shokin-tei's rhythmic planes and their relationships to the garden (207-211).

208

There is no formal hierarchy of space leading to a climax, but rather a gradual movement from dark to light, from higher to lower, from the man-made to the natural — a working outward from precision towards the vague undefined void . . .

Outdoor tea preparation platform (210, 211).

Apparent inconsistencies of scale in the garden at Katsura express the dichotomy in man's relation to his universe — man alone and man in the world. For the garden not only contains elements of human scale — bridges and walks that invite participation and wandering — at the same time it includes elements which convey the feeling of vast, timeless vistas of mountains, islands and the sea — as if our mortal desire for the near, the precise, the closely seen, can be assuaged only by a reminder of the greater reality of the far, the vague, the dimly seen, the transient . . .

Path and bridge leading to the Shokin-tei (212, 205). Stone group at the edge of the pond opposite the Shoin (213). The Shokin-tei and its surrounding garden (214-216, 162, 163).

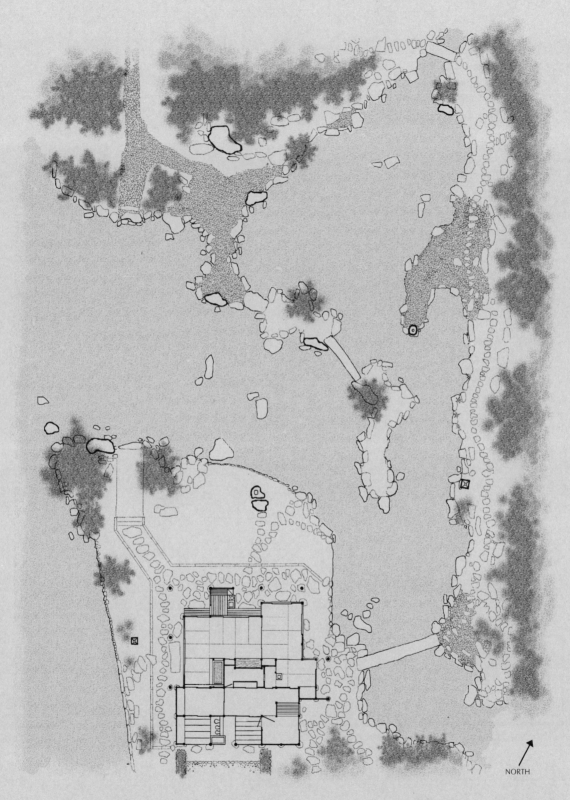

NORTH

KATSURA VILLA, THE SHOKIN-TEI AND GARDEN
SCALE: 1" = 20'

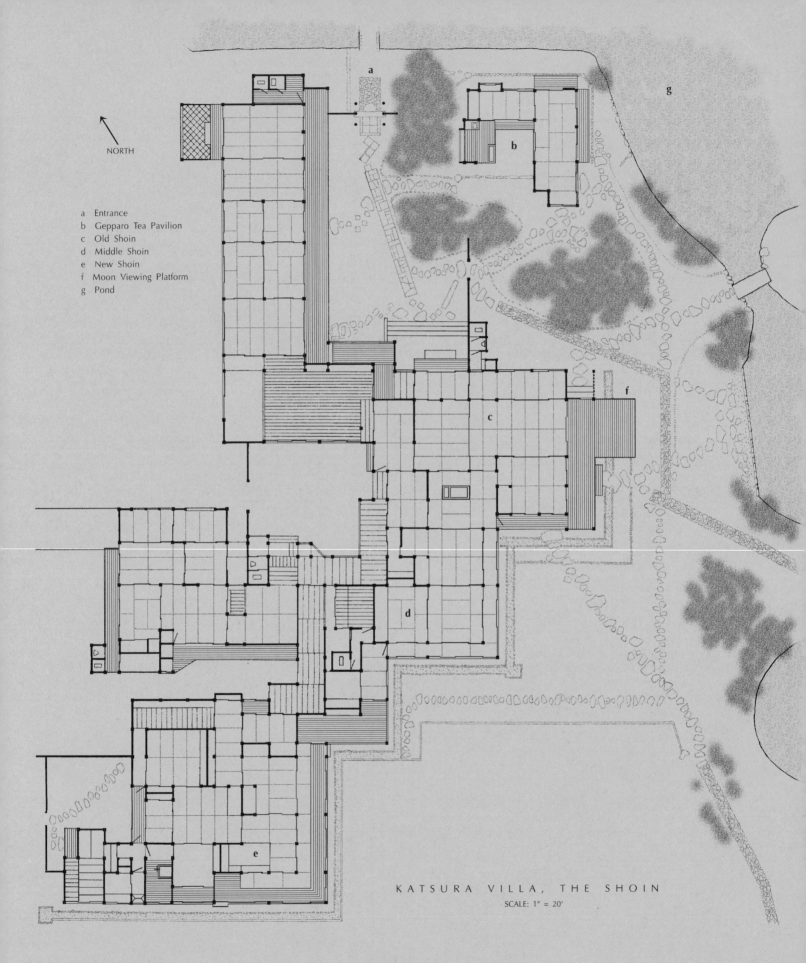

NORTH

a Entrance
b Gepparo Tea Pavilion
c Old Shoin
d Middle Shoin
e New Shoin
f Moon Viewing Platform
g Pond

KATSURA VILLA, THE SHOIN

SCALE: 1" = 20'

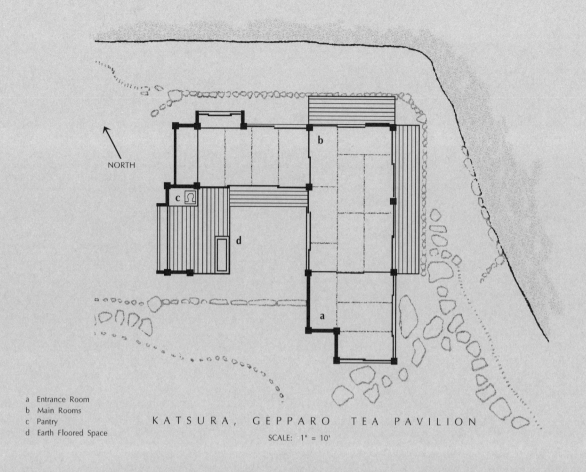

NORTH

a Entrance Room
b Main Rooms
c Pantry
d Earth Floored Space

KATSURA, GEPPARO TEA PAVILION

SCALE: 1" = 10'

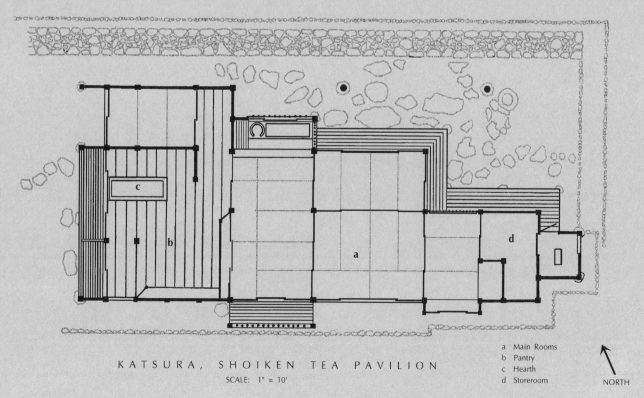

KATSURA, SHOIKEN TEA PAVILION

SCALE: 1" = 10'

a Main Rooms
b Pantry
c Hearth
d Storeroom

NORTH

219

BIBLIOGRAPHY

When the first edition of this book was published there were few books in English on Japanese Architecture. Since that time many books have appeared. I am sure the following short list of books which I find useful overlooks several valuable resources:

Akiyama, Aisaburo, *Shinto & Its Architecture*, Kyoto 1936

Carver, Norman F., Jr., *Japanese Folkhouses*, Kalamazoo, 1984

Itoh, Teiji, *Space and Illusion in the Japanese Garden*, Tokyo 1973

Inoue, Mitsuo, *Space in Japanese Architecture*, Tokyo 1985

Okakura, K., *The Book of Tea*, Tokyo 1931

Suzuki, D., *Zen & Japanese Culture*, Tokyo 1941

Tange, Kenzo, et al, *Ise Prototype of Japanese Architecture*, Tokyo 1965.

Tange, Kenzo, et al, *Katsura, Tradition & Creation in Japanese Architecture*, Tokyo 1960

Taut, Bruno, *Houses & People of Japan*, Tokyo 1937

Yoshida, Tetsuro, *Japanische Architektur*, Tubingen Germany 1952

Yoshida, Tetsuro, *The Japanese House & Garden*, New York, 1955

INDEX

Bold numbers refer to photographs or captions for photographs.

Katsura and Shugakuin are called both Palaces and Villas. Palace is used in the index. The suffixes -jinja and -gu indicate shrines, which are always Shinto, while -ji, -in, -en usually indicate Buddhist temples.

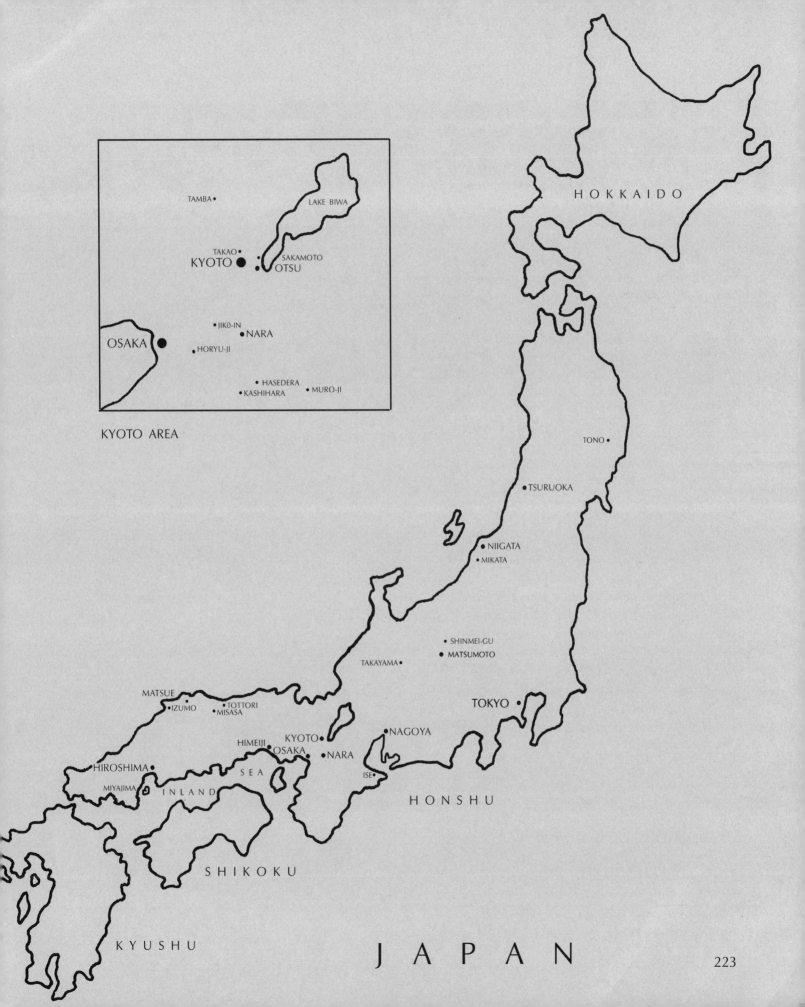

KYOTO AREA

Inset map labels:
TAMBA
LAKE BIWA
TAKAO
SAKAMOTO
KYOTO
OTSU
JIKO-IN
NARA
OSAKA
HORYU-JI
HASEDERA
KASHIHARA
MURO-JI

Main map labels:
HOKKAIDO
TONO
TSURUOKA
NIIGATA
MIKATA
SHINMEI-GU
MATSUMOTO
TAKAYAMA
TOKYO
MATSUE
IZUMO
TOTTORI
MISASA
NAGOYA
HIMEJI
KYOTO
OSAKA
NARA
HIROSHIMA
SEA
ISE
MIYAJIMA
INLAND
HONSHU
SHIKOKU
KYUSHU

J A P A N

223

PRODUCTION NOTES:

Sharp-eyed readers will note a slight change of name from "OF" Japanese Architecture for the orig-inal edition (a better translation of the Japanese title) to "IN" Japanese Architecture.

Except for final scans of the photographs this book was entirely produced on a PC computer (486-33+16mb ram) using Microsoft Word, Page-maker 4.0, and Photoshop for Windows. Proofing was done on an HP-III Laser.

Low resolution scans of either proof sheets or final 8x10s were placed on the page, captions and other text imported from Word, and styles applied. The disks (divided into signature sized files) were given to the printer for film output. High-resolution duotone scans were then stripped in position.

I have been using a computer for writing since the late 1970's, but this is the first time I have designed and output a book totally on the computer. Nothing was ever pasted down, and if I can help it, never will be again.

PHOTOGRAPHIC NOTES:

The original photographs were made during lengthy stays in Japan — a two year period in the 1950's and one year in the 1960's.

The first cameras were twin-lens Rolleiflexes, one for black and white and one for color. Kodak Plus-X film was developed in a wonderful developer, Panthermic 777. It lasted forever becoming the color of strong coffee. Later I had the luxury of a Hasselblad and interchangeable lenses. The Plus-X was developed in D-76. All prints were made recently using Kodak Polygrade.

The Ektachrome color, unfortunately has not held up well. However, several color images for this book were restored using Photoshop.

AVAILABILITY OF PRINTS:

Large archival prints of the images in this book are available from Norman F. Carver, Jr. Prices as of 1993 range from $125 up depending on size. Contact the photographer care of Documan Press, Box 387, Kalamazoo, MI 49005 USA.